The Destruction of the Jaguar
Poems from the Books of Chilam Balam

The Destruction of the Jaguar
Poems from the Books of Chilam Balam

Translated by

Christopher Sawyer-Lauçanno

CITY LIGHTS BOOKS
San Francisco

Copyright © 1987 by Christopher Sawyer-Lauçanno

First published by City Lights Books in 1987

Cover design by Gent Sturgeon

Book designed by Patricia Fujii

Typesetting by Re/Search

Some of these poems appeared in earlier versions in Don
Wellman, ed., *Translations: Experiments in Reading,* Cambridge,
MA: 0.ARS, 1983.

Library of Congress Cataloging-in-Publication Data

Books of Chilam Balam. English. Selections.
  The Destruction of the Jaguar.

  Translation of various Mayan poems from the Books of
Chilam Balam.
  1. Maya poetry—Translations into English.
  2. American poetry—Translations from Maya.
  3. Mayas—History.   4. Mayas—Religion and mythology.
  5. Indians of Mexico—History.   6. Indians of Mexico—Religion
and mythology. I. Sawyer-Lauçanno, Christopher, 1951- .
  II. Title.
PM3968.65.E5B66 1987 897'.4 87–13150
ISBN 0–87286–210–0

CITY LIGHTS BOOKS are edited by Lawrence Ferlinghetti
& Nancy J. Peters and published at the City Lights Bookstore,
261 Columbus Avenue, San Francisco, CA 94133.

*To the memory of Ing. Raymundo García Loera,
in his own way a jaguar priest.*

Contents

Introduction

The Books of Chilam Balam are the only principal surviving sacred texts of the ancient Mayas. Written in the Mayan language but in European script, they are generally considered to be transcriptions and recompilations from memory of material originally contained in the hieroglyphic books, all of which were apparently destroyed by the Spaniards in the early days of the conquest. As they stand now, they are a curious and fascinating combination of prophecy, history, chronology, ritual and mythology with numerous later interpolations and superimpositions of Christian symbolism and belief.

The author of the original work is said to be Chilam Balam who has been identified as a great priest living during the last part of the 15th century. "Chilam," in Mayan, means priest, prophet, mouthpiece of the gods; "balam" means jaguar. Thus Chilam Balam means jaguar priest. Since "Chilam Balam," however, is a fairly standard term of approbation for a powerful prophet, we may be suspicious of the actuality of any particular author. Most likely, the books resulted from the efforts of several hands over several generations. But regardless of their authorship, the texts were held quite sacred by the Mayas, copied and recopied in secret, sequestered in carefully concealed hiding places for more than a century after the conquest.

At present, there are three major Mayan manuscripts, all differing somewhat, and more than a dozen other fragmentary ones. None of these dates from before the late 17th century, but because of the archaic language employed it is assumed that these are copies of much older editions. During the 16th and 17th centuries, in fact, a number of Mayan towns possessed their own *Chilam Balam;* as a result, each extant version is identified with the village in which the manuscript was originally discovered.

Despite the fact that the *Chilam Balam* was written down, it was probably read, even before the conquest, by very few. Instead, it was used as an educational source for young initiates into the priesthood and ceremonially performed. Early Spanish accounts tell of the *Chilam Balam* being sung, danced, chanted and recited to the accompaniment of drums and a variety of wind instruments. In its present form it is extremely difficult, particularly at first glance, to imagine the *Chilam Balam* being performed. Lengthy treatises on the the Mayan calendar are interspersed with Western astrology, ancient prophecies with Christian dogma. In two of the versions a Spanish Romance, written in Mayan, even intrudes into the text. In addition, few passages are logically put into paragraphs or even written in complete sentences and the division of the text into parts seems completely arbitrary. Hidden beneath the garbled sentences and unconnected ramblings, though, there is an evocative imagery of undeniable power, of terrible beauty.

Most of this poetic material is found in the sections dealing with the prophecies. For the ancient Mayas, prophecy was a serious matter, it being devoutly believed that the events of the future had been factually related by the gods to the Chilams, who in turn informed the people. In conjunction with "divine inspiration," the prophets also used history as a guide to the future. For the Mayas, events occurred in cycles, history repeating itself in a continuum. It was possible, as a result, to predict what would happen in a future era by careful study of a similarly demarcated age in the past. The primary unit of time was the "katún," a period of twenty years. Following from this, the prognostications were made katún by katún. A complete cycle consisted of 13 katúns in the following order: 13, 11, 9, 7, 5, 3, 1, 12, 10, 8, 6, 4, 2. It was assumed that once the cycle of 260 years was completed, it would begin again, thus creating the basis for historical divination of the future. Appended to these katún numbers was invariably the Mayan word "Ahau." "Ahau" means ruler or chief and in some of the manuscripts there is an inked portrait of the ruler who is said to govern during the katún.

Although occasionally very specific, most of the predictions have a highly symbolic and metaphoric content. Animals and plants, for example, frequently stand as symbols for something else. The jaguar and eagle most often represent the Mayan rulers or head chiefs; the fox, the Spanish invaders; the deer is an often-used symbol for the Mayan people. Of the plants, the plumeria, a bush or tree with large, highly fragrant white, pink, red or yellow flowers, is associated with lewdness or depravity. Or as the Mayan-Spanish Motul dictionary puts it: "Dishonesty, vicious sins of the flesh and misdeeds of women."

In addition to plant and animal symbols, there are frequent, though often ambiguous references to Christianity. These undoubtedly crept into the texts over the centuries as subsequent Mayan copyists sought to reconcile the ancient beliefs with the new Christian faith. This was not as difficult as it might appear, for many Mayan myths and legends lent themselves to a Christian interpretation. The legend of Kukulcán, itself a superimposition of the Toltec Quetzalcoatl myth on the older Mayan religion, is a good example. According to the Mayas, Kukulcán was a fair-skinned, bearded man/god accredited with introducing new religious practices, including fasting and confession, into Yucatán. Departing from his capital, Chichén Itzá (some sources say betrayed and driven out), he vowed to return one day to reestablish his empire. The ease, by which it was possible to substitute Christ for Kukulcán, is evident. Indeed, many of the Katún prophecies that predicted the return of Kukulcán were simply changed to predict the coming of Christianity.

Despite the obvious attempts to alter the original texts, the *Chilam Balam* is still certainly one of the great pre-Columbian masterpieces. Aside from considerable study by anthropologists, ethnologists and linguists, though, it has never received much attention as an artistic work. Its language, however, in places, is extraordinarily rich in tone and imagery and its portentous evocation of chaos, destruction and death is among the most astonishing in any language, in any time. Neither pure translation nor original work, these versions are instead an attempt to recreate the essence of the ancient texts, to reinvent in a modern idiom the woe and wonder of a gone civilization.

Cambridge-Mérida-Cambridge

Jaguar Priest

A Note on the Sources

I am not a Mayan scholar and my knowledge of the language is severely limited. This book, therefore, needs to be regarded as an artistic work, not as a scholarly one. Indeed, this version would not have been possible without the pioneering efforts of a small but exceedingly dedicated group of scholars who variously managed to collect, preserve, establish, edit and translate the original *Chilam Balam* manuscripts. My work is based primarily on the following editions:

Juan Martínez Hernández, *Chilam Balam de Maní o Códice Pérez,* Mérida: Colegio San José de Artes y Oficios, 1909.

Ermilio Solís Alcalá, *Códice Pérez*, Mérida: Prensa Oriente, 1949.

Ralph Roys, *The Chilam Balam of Chumayel,* Washington, D.C.: The Carnegie Institute of Washington, 1933.

Eugene R. Craine and Reginald C. Reindorp, *The Codex Pérez and the Book of Chilam Balam of Maní,* Norman, OK.: University of Oklahoma Press, 1979.

I am also indebted to Harvard University's Peabody Museum of American Archaeology and Ethnology for allowing me to examine their photographic copy of the *Chilam Balam of Maní*. Also indispensible were the following:

Alfred M. Tozzer, *A Maya Grammar,* New York: Dover, 1977.

Juan Pio Perez, *Diccionario de la lengua Maya,* Mérida, 1877.

Diccionario de Motul: Maya-Español (16th Century) first discovered and published by Martínez Hernández in 1929 in Mérida.

From the Spanish Chronicles of Bishop Diego de Landa

The Indians sadly received the yoke of slavery. And although the Spaniards had the country well divided and under control, the Indians were not lacking for trouble-makers who tried to incite them, resulting in cruel chastisements which caused, in turn, a decrease in the native population. They burned alive some principal lords in Cupal province and hanged others. A charge was levied against Yobain, the town of the Chels, and they seized the leaders and put them in chains in a house and set it afire, burning them with the greatest inhumanity in the world.

And I, Diego de Landa, saw a tree near this town on which the captain hanged many Indian women from the branches and hanged their children by the feet. And in this same town and in another called Verey, two leagues from there, they hanged two Indian women, one a virgin, and the other newly-married, for no other crime than that they were beautiful and feared that the Spanish camp would be disturbed by them. By doing this they showed the Indians that the Spaniards were not interested in their women. These two are not forgotten, neither by the Indians nor the Spanish, but are remembered still for their great beauty and for the cruel way in which they were killed.

And when the Indians in the provinces of Cochua and Chetumal revolted, the Spaniards put down the rebellion in such a way that these provinces, once the most thickly settled, became the least populated of any in the country. They committed unheard-of cruelties, cutting off hands, noses, arms and legs, cutting off the breasts of women and throwing the women themselves into deep lagoons with gourds tied to their feet. And they stabbed the little children because they could not walk as fast as their mothers. And if those who walked chained together by the neck became ill, or didn't move as fast as the others, they cut off their heads so that they wouldn't have to stop and unchain them. The great number of women captives in the procession were treated the same way as the men.

from Diego de Landa, *Relación de las Cosas de Yucatán*, c. 1566, translation by Christopher Sawyer-Lauçanno

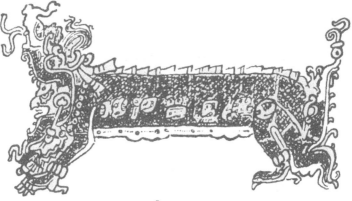

Itzamna
(The great earth monster.)
Dresden Codex

CATECHISM

From where do they come,
the sacred books?
From Hun Ahau
the god of death
the god of the morning star.

And how did they come?
They came with him
when he ascended from Metnal
to Mount Chun-Caan.

And to whom were they given?
To Chilam Balam and Xupan Nauat
our clear-eyed prophets,
our fierce jaguar priests.

And what do they say?
They foretell the future
katún by katún,
era by era,
foretell the Maya's suffering
foretell the anguish,
foretell the murder,
foretell the foreigners' coming.

THE PROPHECIES RECEIVED

I

To the small house of Nacom Balam
the five great priests came.
First, Chilam Balam, the prophet of Maní
then Napuctun, the wise, the wizened
next, Xupan Nauat and Kauil Chel
fearless guardians of the holy books,
the seven sacred texts of the city of Uxmal,
and finally too, old Nahau Pech
the ageless sage of Mayapán.

They came that night those jaguar priests,
came clad in white,
in the garments of Kukulcán,
came then into the holy one's house
into the house of Nacom Balam.

Came too that night into that house
the greatest of Gods, Hunab-Ku,
came also that night, his awesome escorts,
the thirteen gods, Oxlahun-Ti-Ku
and the thousand gods, Hun-Pic-Ti-Ku.
Came that night into that house those gods.

II

On new mats sat
the holy men
waiting for a sign
from Nacom Balam
from Hunab-Ku
or from his escorts.
They watched the fire,
waited.
Talked in whispers,
waited.
Then, suddenly
Nacom Balam
twisted,
rose
into mid-air
slowly, steadily
hovered there,
the orange light
transfixing him.
Then, graceful
as a young puma,
he descended to his mat
lay still for one
brief moment,
his gray eyes glazed,
breathing fierce,
palms extended.

From his body
came then the voice
sliding over his obsidian teeth,
at first, just a murmur,
then a low hum,
then these words:

"Know this my priests,
know that soon
a katún shall come
that will mark
the beginning of the end
of all our ways.

"Know that you here
are the first
to know this future.
Know that
after three moons
over the nine mountains,
the judge of the bull will come
with money or white wax
with a cross that will conquer
that will trample our laws,
our justice, our people.
The quetzal will lose its plumes,
the eagle its claws.

"Know that in the new era
the jaguar will have a rabbit's body,
broken teeth,
a spear of sorrow piercing its side.
The rulers will lose their mats,
their white clothes,
will wander the streets as mangy dogs.
The people will gnaw roots,
eat the leaves of weeds
and in the cities
the vultures will grow fat
on the cadavers.

"The new governors
will lie and cheat and steal.
Girls will have children
like chickens.
Like dying deer
the once bold and once brave
will scatter into the forests,
flee Mayapán, Ziyancaan
and all our lands.

"In the era after
heads will bow to foreign priests,
to alien gods,
to barbarous rulers.
Those who live
will live as half men,

their heads locked in stocks.
It will be a time of evil,
of constant thunder,
an era when tame beasts bite,
the wise become dunces,
the prophets blind.

"The end of this katún
will be the end of all katúns,
the end of history.
Remember these words, holy men
remember these bitter words
of the one true god
come from heaven.
Remember his counsel
when the last son of the Itzás
lies buried in a shallow grave,
his liver plucked by vultures,
his eyes pecked out by crows."

III
Those sacred prophecies
drifted in the orange air
entwining with the fire
glowing, growing in the shadows.
The priests sat,
the silence alive

with their soundless sighs,
by the cadence of their hearts
beating in their brains.

Then old Nacom Balam
rose from the floor,
face white as a new lily,
eyes no longer glazed.

THE PROPHECIES DELIVERED
TO THE PEOPLE

Napuctun Speaks

Burn, burn, burn
on earth we shall burn
become cinders in
the blowing wind
drift over the land
over the mountains
out to sea.

What has been written
will be fulfilled.
What has been spoken
will come to be.

Weep, weep, weep
but know,
know well:
Ash does not suffer.

Ah Kauil Chel Speaks

What has been written
will be fulfilled.

Though you may not comprehend it
though you may not understand it
he will come who knows
how the ages unfold
one unto another
like the stone steps
on the palace of the governor.

For now
the priests, the prophets
will interpret
what is to be fulfilled,
shall herald with sorrow
the destruction of the jaguar.

Nahau Pech Speaks

Four katúns will pass,
four katúns of terror,
the snakes strangling themselves,
the great muddy alligator
led about on a rope
the macaw gorging
on Mayan flesh.

Four katúns will pass
before pity returns,
before the bearer
of a foreign god
will arrive.

Weep Itzás
weep when you remember
what I have spoken.

Xupan Nauat Speaks

Brothers, prepare yourselves.
Make ready for the arrival
of the man with visor,
roaring stick, gaping jaws
and bloody teeth.
Make ready for the humiliation
of the jaguar and the eagle
for the plague of ants
for the defeat of our rulers
who have governed
since the world began.

Prepare yourselves
to carry, like turtles,
your house upon your back
to surrender your white clothes
to see before your eyes
white stone turn to powder,
order evaporate like dew.
Prepare yourselves
to endure like dogs
panting with open mouths,
to live like ferrets
hiding in hollowed logs.

He comes to kill,
to infect with wars,
to spread pestilence
and unending famine.
He comes to destroy
the jaguar and the puma
to raze the sacred houses
to pluck the quetzal's plumes.
He comes to scatter
all of the great priests,
to hunt down Hunab-Ku,
pierce his side with spears,
to burn even
these sacred books
the prophecies of Hunab-Ku,
these holy texts
which speak my speech.

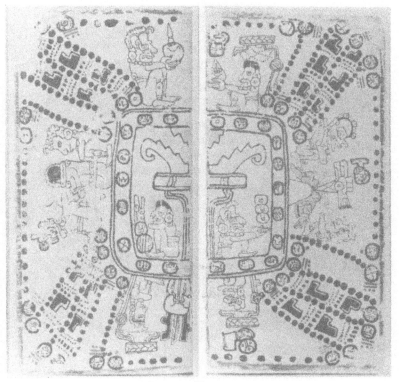

Four world quarters
Madrid Codex

Llaman a esta
cuenta en su lengua
Vazlizonkatam que
quiere dezir La cuenta de
Los Katunes.

Katún Wheel
(after Landa)

THE KATÚN PROPHECIES

Katún 13 Ahau

All that shall pass
is written on the petals
of the flower and
on the great stone at Mayapán.
It is the katún
of great Itzamna
ruler of the cosmos,
of great wars in heaven:
The sun swallows the moon
and the moon, the sun.
The earth at noon
will be as dark
as at midnight
foretelling the end of order.

For five years
the crops will not grow,
even the locusts
will starve,
fall to the ground
to be eaten like delicacies.

The governors and prophets
will always be drunk
and foreign lords
and foreign priests
will come to tear the mats
from under their bloated bodies.

The cornfield workers
will go mad, mutter lies
to themselves
and bury the rulers
they've known since birth.
Their children will know nothing,
will wander the streets
not recognizing their parents.
The girls will sell themselves,
the wives and husbands
take lovers,
heedless of the old laws,
of the prescribed ways.

The foreign men with big boots
will be on their mats
or lounge all day in bed
ignorant and perverted,
quarreling among themselves.

The roar of the jaguar
will be silenced
by the cruel trap,
the cry of the deer
will be long and tender
echo through the forest
until it too is finally
and forever stilled.

Katún 11 Ahau

Into this katún march
the strangers with red beards,
white skin and treacherous eyes.
It is the dawn
of the jaguar's misery
of the suffering of the people
of the end to plenty.
It is the first night
of the last days of the world.

Oh Itzá make ready!
Look for the white circle in the sky,
for the wooden staff that descends
from the thirteen heavens,
for the white messenger bird
of the great Kukulcán.
Listen to the mut-bird's cry
listen to the sorrowful wail
that catches in his throat
choking the sweet song of past days.

Oh Itzá make ready!
In this era they come
with flames at their fingertips
with poison, with stout ropes
for hanging the lords,

with rage without reason
with blood thirst
in their treacherous hearts.

Oh Itzá make ready!
Your villages will be turned
into piles of rubble,
your monuments broken,
your gods desecrated
hurled from the temple top.
Prayer is useless
before the fire
before the fury
of the invaders' swords.
Prepare yourselves
to become handmaids
to the evil conquerors
to build new villages
with sticks and stones,
villages in which you are slaves.

Oh Itzá, prepare yourselves
for the whips
for the thorns
for the fire
for the fire
for the fire.

Katún 9 Ahau

It is the era
of the impotent jaguar
of the headless deer
of the blind parrot
of the legless monkey.
Even at night
the screech owls cower
not venturing forth
in search of prey.

It is the era
of the conqueror
and the conquered
of pillage and ruin and waste,
the gods driven underground
and buried
in the minds
of a few old men gone mad.

No harvest
no corn
only black bread
and corpses hanging from trees
in autumn light.
It is the era prophesied
by Ah Kauil Chel
the sage priest of Uxmal:

"Oh lord, at this era's end
though it be bitter to know
he will come and reward you
for rolling up his mat
and with him, from everywhere
will come the plagues
the age of lamentation.

"No priest nor fortune teller
can read the signs.
Chaos rules on earth."

The drum and rattle of Katún 7.
(from a stele in Belize)
(after T. Gann)

Katún 7 Ahau

Drum and rattle
fornication and drunkenness
and the wild plumeria.
Plumeria, the katún's bread
plumeria, its water
plumeria, its wine.

Here begins the depravity
of the wise men,
here begins the beckoning
of rot and stench and fuck.

Fuck is the katún's face.
Fuck is its sandal.
Fuck is its head.
Fuck is its gait.

From his bed
the governor rules,
bathes priest and prophet
in rose water,
feeds them pink bread.

The water jugs
are filled to overflowing
and the market stalls

piled high with fruit,
beans, squash, corn, new bread.
But there is only an appetite
for lust and greed and fuck.

Men, women, children, chiefs
judges, lords, clerks, workers,
people great and small
twist their mouths
wink their eyes
drool at the lips.

All teaching is lost.
All shame is lost.
The head chiefs are hanged.
The prophets are hanged.
The priests are hanged.

The katún limps forth
on three legs
made weak by fuck
by drink, by ignorance,
by a loss of the old ways.

Katún 5 Ahau

Harsh is the face
harsh is the message
of this katún.
The diviner shakes
his bloody rattle,
the stinging ants
pour forth,
the moon is mutilated,
infants butchered,
and devoured
like suckling pigs.
The face of Kauil,
lord of the four
changing heavens
is made blind as stone.

It is the katún
of the two-day kings,
of the opossum chief,
the fox chief,
the mosquito chief,
the scorpion chief.
It is the time
of the plumeria throne
of the ambush by Totil-och,

the burrowing opossum
who crouches and waits
until the moment is ripe
to enter the marketplace.

It is the katún
of deception and disorder.
The kinkajou claws
the jaguar's back,
the turtle forsakes his shell.
There is treachery
and more treachery.
There are hangings
and more hangings.
Chiefs greedy for dominion
scourge the land,
dictate for a day,
then fall.

Then, from over the hills
like a batallion of ants
come the warriors from Uaymil,
the deliverers of the sad Maya
seeking their vengeance
against the world.

Katún 3 Ahau

Know by these signs
the coming of the katún:
flames sprouting
from a goat's horn,
the jaguar spreading
his skin in the marketplace,
the dog drinking
from stagnant pools.

Though the rains come
they are white rains,
rains from rabbit skies,
rains from woodpecker skies,
from vulture skies,
from deer skies.
The palm frond,
three times erected
falls in a clatter
on the bare stones
heralding the locusts' arrival.

It is an age of quarrels
and of havoc at the crossroads,
of new towns built
and old ones abandoned.

The people move
as if in dreams
waiting for miracles.
They choke themselves,
vomit what they swallow
and stand all day
in the sun giving thanks
for their poor nourishment.

In his bed the governor weeps,
does not recognize
his kinsmen or his parents.
The lion cubs stride
brazenly into the city,
pick clean the bones
that lie in the vomit.

On the edge of the forest
the red, white and gray foxes
howl long into the night,
mock the hunters
worshipping an alien god.

◦ 🝙 *Katún 1 Ahau*

The owls descend
from the ruins,
salt and rope
from the sky.
The lords govern
like common fools:
weak, ignorant, insolent,
their eyes turned upward.

A new throne is set up
in Ichcaanzihoo,
city of the bald beggars
where even the new governor
in his borrowed kingdom
rules from a borrowed mat,
sleeps in a borrowed bed
and is easily dethroned.

Vagabonds roam aimless
through the city streets,
pledge allegiance
to any lord
and to no lord.
The people are all prisoners,
turtledoves tied together
with rope and shame.

Katún 12 Ahau

Songs of beauty
poems of courage,
carved jade,
rubies set in gold.
For a time there is peace.
For a time there are great works.
Kings and caciques
nobles and subjects
are all content.
There is bread
in the market,
corn in the fields.

Then from Tibalam
where once the governors ruled
comes the foreign fox
who surprises the priests,
the lords on their mats.
With indifference
he slaughters
brave warriors,
ancient priests,
old women and virgins
and helpless children.

28

Into the forests
the Mayas will flee
take their beds and mats
forage like starving deer.
In the once great cities
the sly fox
rules with ease
seated on the bloody backs
of fallen warriors.
Slowly and carefully
he pulls the claws
from the mighty jaguar.

Katún 10 Ahau

Desperation and drought
and always the sun
turning the green hills brown.
Even in the deep forests
there is no refuge:
The birds' nests become kindling,
the trees, logs for the fire.
The hooves of the deer burn,
the lake water scalds,
the sand by the sea
glows with white heat
and even the rocks splinter
from the sun's relentless ardor.

The homeless birds do not sing
and the jaguars
lie listless
at the mouths of caves.
The drum and bell
call the people to dine
on burnt tree bark
and the governors,
white men with pale eyes
do nothing
but scratch their beards
and seek shade.

It is a sad katún,
a katún of misery
and slow death,
an age when
the sorrowful Mayas
long for an end
to the world.
The great Bacabs
at the four world quarters
seek too its destruction,
tear at one another
but destroy only beehives.
The misery goes on
day after night after day
goes on and on
patiently punishing the earth
and all its mournful children.

:❘▯▯ *Katún 8 Ahau*

And Lord Lahun Chan
his eyes wet with tears
goes forth
onto the arid plain
to beg from the gods
hard bread and water
that his people might live.

It is the era
when neither bread nor water
can be found
not on the plain
not in the forests
not in the whole world.
It is the era
when the animals scatter,
chill winds driving them south,
drought gnawing their tails.

And the great god
Kinich Kakmo comes down
from the summit of heaven
leaves his throne, his mat, his comfort
comes onto the plain
to scold his bad children

in Chichén Itzá
and in the north coast kingdoms
to demand a stop to their quarrels,
their bickering among themselves
or let them prepare for the days
of stones and blood.

And his children
cry out to the Itzás
that with the coming of the cross
their kingdoms will fall
their governors will fall
that even Kinich Kakmo will fall,
the trees become scaffolds
bearing only the fruit
of hanged men.

So it is foretold
in the old books
of the jaguar priests.

*⊞ *Katún 6 Ahau*

Proud rulers
on dias and mat
Uxmal and Kinich Kakmo
go out at night
and pray to the stars
and to the heavens
asking the way
for deliverance from decay
asking for things to be
as they were
in the old days.

It is a time of war,
a time of famine.
Having no corn
the people make bread
from the ramón tree,
eat grass and rocks
and die.

The jaguar flees
and the quetzal too.
Delusion descends.
Even the governors
cannot remember
how the world began

and for the third time
the people war with stones.
Those who return
return with heads wrapped
in bloody bandages,
holes for eyes,
stumps for legs.

They weep,
cry out for an end to unreason,
cry out for release from the prophecy,
cry out for release from the future.

Katún 4 Ahau

Awakening at dawn
finding their faces staring southward
the cornfield workers know
the era is half over,
know the rain will fall no more
that the corn will not grow
that the gourd trees
will shrivel in the hot wind.

They weep,
their faces cracking
their eyes glowing with death.
Weep for water
trade their white garments for bread
talk of the plague of ants
that descends on the beehives
talk of decay
that sweeps the land.

The governors,
their mats facing westward,
talk as deaf men
hearing nothing
hearing no one.
They too know that soon

the foreign lords will come
leading death's parade.
They too know that spring
will bring the singing quetzal
the vomiting of blood
and the tribute pouch strapped
to a horse's hind
to be filled
with jewels and gold
got by blood,
with bread.

⬚ *Katún 2 Ahau*

So much slaughter,
so much death.
The stench of corpses
fouls the clean air.
The maggots burrow
into the marrow
of the lucky dead
piled as high
as the great temple.
The furnaces will blaze
all day and all night
burning the rot,
and green smoke
will fill even
the most distant valleys.

The great lord
will have his mat and dias,
his bread and water
but he will be
as powerless as a fawn
against the savage
black-bearded invaders.
Soon they will rule,

take the widows and girls
of the dead warriors
into their houses
dress them in foreign clothes
teach them the foreign tongue
and the foreign ways.

The proud Mayan blood
will turn tainted with whiteness,
the children
of once-great warriors
will be slaves and whores
and handymen and servants
to the conquerors,
betray their fallen
fathers and grandfathers,
become vultures
preying on their own kind.

PROPHECIES FOR THE TURN
OF THE YEAR

If the new year
begins on a Sunday
there will be great drought
and four terrible plagues.
For half the year
the wind will blow
cold and harsh
from the north,
for the other half,
the sun will blaze
turning the lakes
into mud flats,
the mighty river
into a small brook.
The trees will not flower
the fruits will wither
on the dry branches.
The great and the small
will be brought together
through shared hunger
and even the bees
will desert the parched land.
The unbelievers will want war
but it must not be.

If the new year
begins on a Monday
only the strong
will know good days
for the gods will punish
the sad Mayas
with torrents of rain.
Cold will invade
even the palace
and the bees
will die in mid-air,
the honey go bad.
In cramped cold corners
the timid will crouch
and on the side of the road
the people will die
waiting for the sun.

If the new year
begins on a Tuesday
it will be a year
of quarrels and rancour
of fog and drought
of hunger and poverty.
What little corn there is
will not be sold—

no one will have money
or goods to trade
and Hun Ahau, the god of death
will gather many in Metnal
where dwell the dead,
will gather even the nobles
and great lords and prophets.

If the new year
begins on Wednesday
there will be
just enough rain
and no ill winds
and warm skies.
Even the servants
will live well
and become arrogant
at their good fortune.
Travelers, though, will die
beside the roads
and many of the young
will also perish.
There will be few virgins
and their numbers
will dwindle further

because of bestial men
who will carry them off
only to leave them bleeding
and full of disease.

If the new year
begins on a Thursday
it will be a year
of drought and desolation.
The tongues of animals and men
will swell for lack of water.
The trees will not bloom,
the crops will be scorched
and the wild fruit
will shrivel on the branch
and on the vine.
Neither spears nor arrows
can defend the mighty Mayas
against Death's dark warriors.

If the new year
begins on a Friday
the sun will shine
even through the rain
turning the fields
to fine powder

and the wind will blow
the seeds into the sea
and into the forests.
Pestilence will walk the earth
and many will denounce
the great gods,
form packs of unbelievers
causing illness to descend
with even greater fury
on the heads
of the afflicted Maya.

Translator's note: .
The prediction for Saturday is missing
in all of the extant copies of the *Chilam Balam.*

THE TUN WHEEL

The wheel of time turns,
foretells the future
tells the past.

Turns in the sun
and in the shadow.
Turns through the long night.

Counts off the days
and the years
and all the epochs

gives us the signs,
the ones to live by
and those to die by.

Carries us up the ninefold path
shows us the nine precious gifts
brings us face to face with the gods

guides us in our perilous journeys
teaches us of demons
who preside over the darkness.

Brings us to the awesome
reckoning with the rose
on whose petals are inscribed

the book of years,
the eternal turning
towards our ends.

WHAT THE THUNDER SAYS

If it thunders on Sunday,
the sun's sacred day
it is a sign
that death's destroyers
come again to earth
come again to hunt down
the priests and teachers
to rip out their hearts
to feed gluttonously
on their souls.

If it thunders on Monday,
the moon's sacred day
it means a time
of warriors
of blood
of beastly butchery.
Though the trees blossom
poison lingers in the fruit.

If it thunders on Tuesday,
or if the moon swallows the sun
or the sun the moon
or if the evil stars
lurk in the heavens,
it foretells famine,
the trees withering
the fruit turning to dust.

If it thunders on Wednesday,
or if the moon feasts on the sun
or the sun on the moon
then great evil will be unleashed
will rampage across the fields
will enter the villages
crawl under the mats
perch in the roofbeams
ambush even the pious.

If it thunders on Thursday,
it foretells a good harvest
of trees pregnant with fruit.
In the hills
the farmers will rejoice,
in the cities
the people will sing praises
dance dances by firelight
pay homage to the good, great gods.

If it thunders on Friday,
or if the sun enshrouds the moon
or the moon the sun
it is a sign of terrible things,
of fierce misfortune
all over the earth:
The lords will be brought down

plagues will fall on the people
wars will be waged between villages
between governors
between valiant commanders.
Even the law courts
will be in disarray.

If it thunders on Saturday,
the ringed planet's sacred day
or if the sun or moon
fall into darkness
or long shadow,
it is a sign
that both evil and war
will possess the earth,
rule over the people,
litter the land with victims.

CREATION OF THE WORLD

For every destruction, a creation
for every creation, a destruction.
In every birth a death,
in every death a birth.
This is the way it has been.
This is the way it will be.

Listen, listen well
it is most important to know this,
most important to believe this
for this is the history of the world
the story of how it was
in the twilight between
nothing and something
in the days after the flood
in the days after the sky had fallen
in the time before the jaguar throne,
before the building of the great cities
before even the cornfields.

I speak to you now
of a spectral time
when no world hung
between the thirteen heavens
and the nine cold hells.

I speak to you now
of Oxlahun-Ti-Ku,
god of the thirteen heavens
and of Bolon-Ti-Ku,
god of the nine hells
of how they created
the world and all life
and then destroyed it again
by washing the world in water
and of how Oxlahan-Ti-Ku
slit the throat
of the great earth crocodile,
Itzam-Cab-Ain, and with his body
formed the Peten, land of the Mayas.

And I speak to you now
of Ah Muzencab, god of the bees
and of his treachery
of how he bound the eyes
of mighty Oxlahan-Ti-Ku
god of the thirteen heavens,
how he left him prey
for Bolon-Ti-Ku
who ascended from his nine hells
to seize Oxlahan-Ti-Ku
to smash in his head
to spit in his face
to steal his sceptre
and his sacred ash.

Things were dark then:
Oxlahan-Ti-Ku lay on his back
like a captive turtle
and bellowed into the blackness,
called down fire from the skies
and rocks and stones and clubs.
Once freed, he took
shoots of the Yaxun tree,
large and small gourd seeds
and wrapped them
in the body of the earth god
Bolon Dz'acab, then took the hearts
of squash seeds and ascended
back to his sacred throne
high in the thirteen heavens.

And upon the earth the evil betrayers
were buried alive, but without
their hearts beating in them.
And those on the strand
were drowned in an avalanche of waves
which swept over all the land
turning it into one vast sea.

And then it was that
the four Bacabs were set up
one at each corner of the world.
Fierce guardians, their arms raised

they hold the world
dangling between the nine hells
and the thirteen heavens.
Then, after this,
they placed first in the east
the red ceiba tree
and upon this red tree of abundance
was set up the red cock oriole.
Then the white ceiba tree
the white tree of abundance
was placed in the north
for the white breasted pixoy to perch on.
And in the west
was set up the black ceiba tree
the black tree of abundance
for the black-crested pixoy
to perch upon.
And in the south
was placed the yellow ceiba tree
and in its branches
sat the yellow-breasted pixoy,
the yellow cock oriole and the timid mut-bird.

Then finally, in the center of the world,
was placed the great green ceiba,
the great, green tree of abundance
whose branches rise
into the thirteen heavens,

whose roots twist around
the guts of the world.

But still it was not finished.

Next, at each corner of the world
was set up a great stone.
In the west, a red one
to guide people to the lord,
in the north, a white one,
to show also the way to the palace.
And in the west was set up
Lahun Chan, to bear gifts
to the lord and in the south
a yellow stone was set up
to show the messengers the road.

And over the whole world
was set up Ah Uuc Cheknal,
he who fertilizes the maize seven times.
He came from the earth's seventh stratum
to fecundate great Itzam-Cab-Ain,
the terrible earth monster
with the body of a whale
and the head and feet of a crocodile.
And when he did this

the heavens themselves
rubbed against the belly of the earth.
Among the four torches,
among the four layers of stars
they writhed and roared
until the world came forth.

FLIGHT OF THE ITZÁS

They came with a fury
with a rage without reason
with a thirst for blood,
for heads, for jewels.
Came into our lands
to conquer for no quarrel
to seize for the sake of seizing
to claim for an absent king
our lands, our corn, our people.

They came from the east,
those foreign lords,
came to the village of Nacom Balam,
took the town and the people
and the fields and the trees
and even the great black crows.

Then the Itzá went away,
left by the thousands.
Thirteen measures of corn
they had per head,
and nine measures and
three handfuls of grain.

And many of the magicians
from the town went with them
and many of the town's daughters
formed their growing troop.
They did not want to join
the treacherous foreigners,
did not want to bow
to a foreign god,
did not want to pay tribute
to a foreign lord.
They guarded their birds
and their stones,
their jaguars and
their three magic emblems
and fled with spears
deep into the dense forest.

Before the conquerors came
there was no sin,
no sickness, no aches,
no fevers, no pox.
The foreigners stood
the world on its head,
made day become night.
There were no longer

any lucky days
after they came into our lands.
There was no more sound judgement,
no more great vision.
The great teachers never came again
nor any great priests,
just death and blood
and sorrow, sorrow, sorrow!

From the Spanish Chronicles of Bishop Diego de Landa

If it was the devil who put together this compilation of the katúns, he did it, as usual, to glorify himself, or if it was a man, he must have been a great idolator because with these katúns he added to all the principal tricks and omens and deceptions by which these people, in their miseries, were totally deceived. And although this was the science to which they gave the most credit and credence, not even all the priests knew how to interpret it . . . We found a large number of these books of characters, but since they contained nothing but superstition and lies of the devil, we burned them all which caused them tremendous anguish and pain.

from Diego de Landa, *Relación de las Cosas de Yucatán*, c. 1566, translation by Christopher Sawyer-Lauçanno

9 780872 862104